MINI-GUIDES

D-DAY IN NORMANDY........

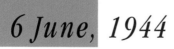

6 June, 1944

Alexandre THERS

Lay-out by the author - Computer graphics by Yann-Erwin ROBERT
Translated from the French by Jonathan NORTH

h&c
PARIS

THEY ARE COMING!

On the evening of June 5, 1944 some 24,000 Allied airborne troops assembled at 22 airfields scattered across southern England. The men, loaded with equipment and with blackened faces, clambered aboard transport planes and gliders. The first planes took off at 21.30. These men, the vanguard of the liberating army, were to land behind the Norman coast, spread confusion in the German ranks and obstruct their movement, then act in support of the main Allied force due to land the following day.

Operation Overlord

German setbacks on all fronts in 1943 persuaded the Allies that a landing in Western Europe would now meet with success. Such an operation had long been requested by the Soviet Union which hoped that her allies would thus decisively support the Soviet offensive in the east. To this end the Allies began the concentration of hundreds of thousands of men in the southern counties of England whilst also deploying boats, readying tanks and supplying millions of tons of supplies. General Dwight Eisenhower was appointed to the role of Supreme Commander of Allied Forces in December 1943 and to him fell the responsibility of organizing the amphibious assault.

The training of the troops began in early 1944. Crews familiarized themselves with amphibious Shermans (Duplex Drive, or DDs, known to the troops as Donald Ducks), whilst demolition teams practiced overcoming mined obstacles. Every effort was poured into this giant campaign directed at north-west Europe. It would be given the name Operation Overlord whilst the naval assault bore the name Operation Neptune.

Newbury, England, late June 5, 1944. Eisenhower, smiling but evidently tense, chats with soldiers of the 502nd Parachute Infantry Regiment (101st Airborne Div.) before they embark on their mission. Their morale was extremely high. (National Archives)

British paratrooper's wings, worn by qualified troopers assigned to parachute units. (Militaria Magazine)

Bottom right : an American infantryman training in Great Britain. He carries a pole charge of 10 TNT blocks. The array of defenses and obstacles the troops would encounter had been minutely studied in order to find the best way of destroying them. (National Archives)

A 1/2 pound block of TNT, issued to blow a foxhole on the beach and to make up various destruction charges. (Militaria Magazine)

But one significant problem remained. Where should the Allies land? The ideal place had to fit some precise criteria. It had to be within a comfortable range for the Allies, especially for their fighter aircraft, and have suitable ports for the massive influx of men and equipment. The landing site had to fall somewhere between the Pas-de-Calais and Normandy. The Pas-de-Calais seemed to be the best option as it was the closest to the English coast but, for that reason alone, it was the best defended. Its high cliffs, narrow beaches and lack of suitable ports also posed problems. Normandy, on the other hand, with its vast beaches, long coastline, and numerous ports was more difficult to defend. Normandy was selected.

The Forces Deploy

The Allies mustered 195,701 men for Operation Neptune and these were embarked on warships and transports. Land forces were assigned to Montgomery's 21st Army Group, comprising the 1st (US) Army under Bradley and the 2nd (British) Army under Dempsey.

Above: British paratroopers climb aboard an Albemarle troop carrying plane.
(IWM)

At 22.00 on June 5, 1944, this Canadian pathfinder checks his watch before boarding an aircraft at Harwell in England. He belongs to Company C of the 1st Canadian Paratroop Battalion (6th Airborne Division). (Reconstruction by Militaria Magazine)

The Atlantic Wall as seen through the eyes of German propaganda. The defenses stretched 120 miles from Le Havre to Barfleur but only boasted 18 batteries of coastal artillery. Twelve of these were out of range of the landing beaches. (DR)

American Rear Admiral Kirk, commanded the Western Task Force, given the task of protecting and supporting the landings. The British Admiral, Bertram Ramsay, commanded all the naval forces engaged in supporting the invasion. (National Archives)

....

A British cruiser. There were 105 British, American, French and Dutch warships involved in D-Day. But the initial bombardment did not live up to expectations. (DR)

Airborne forces numbered some 24,000 men. In addition, there were 5,050 fighters, 3,460 heavy bombers, 1,650 light and medium bombers, 2,310 transport planes, 2,600 gliders and 700 reconnaissance planes to support the task force. These were organized into the 8th and 9th (US) Airforce and the 2nd (British) Tactical Airforce. The fleet which would transport the host across the Channel comprised 1,213 warships, 4,126 landing craft, 736 supply vessels and 864 merchantmen. There was an American fleet, the Western Task Force under Rear Admiral Alan G. Kirk and a British fleet, the Eastern Task Force, under Admiral Bertram H. Ramsay.

The Germans could call upon their 7th and 15th Armies, part of Rommel's Army Group. Generaloberst Friedrich B. Dollmann's 7th Army consisted of the 84th Corps: the 243rd, 709th, 91st, 352nd, 716th and 77th Infantry Divisions. There was also the 6th Parachute Regiment as well as the 319th Infantry Division based in the Channel Islands. Generaloberst Hans von Salmuth's 15th Army was based around his 81st Corps: the 346th, 711th and 245th Infantry Divisions as well as the 17th Luftwaffe Field Division. Inland he also had the 84th Infantry Division. These units relied, in

part, on battalions drawn from the ranks of Soviet prisoners of war. The 21st Panzer Division, 12th SS (Hitlerjugend) Division and the Panzer Lehr Division were kept in reserve. Finally, the 3rd Luftflotte formed the core of the aerial defense with 419 planes of all types.

The German Defenses

Such a vast concentration of Allied troops in the southern counties of England could not hope to escape the notice of the Germans and they had done as much as they could to strengthen their defenses on the French coast. Rommel's arrival as commander of Army

SS-Standartenführer Kurt Meyer (left) talks to Feldmarschall von Rundstedt whilst Fritz Witt, commander of the 12th SS Panzer Division, looks on. Rommel counted on tanks to provide the backbone of the German counterattack. He hoped to be able to use Panzergruppe West, von Rundstedt's reserve, but he hoped in vain. (DR)

Below : the Germans liberally scattered all kinds of explosives on the beaches. This is a concrete Stockmine. (Private Collection)

British Spitfire fighters were sometimes used to fly photographic reconnaissance missions over a coast still being reinforced by the enemy. (Model built by Anis Elbied/ WingMasters)

A German propaganda poster used widely in Normandy which conjures up the image of Joan of Arc to stigmatize the British bombers. (DR)

Group B in January 1944 added a new impetus to these preparations. Soon the coastline bristled with a whole range of obstacles: stakes (roughly every third stake had a land mine secured to the top), 'hedgehogs' constructed out of steel girders, and ramps. These obstacles were reinforced by lines of antitank trenches, barbed wire, casemates and artillery posts. Inland fields and meadows were dotted with sharpened stakes, the so-called Rommel Asparagus, designed to prevent Allied gliders from landing.

Operation Neptune

On the morning of June 5, 1944, some 5,339 vessels took to the sea and took up position off the French coast. The morning of June 6 dawned to a rough sea. The Allies had selected a stretch of coast 50 miles long and split it into five sections. To the west the Americans were to land on Utah and Omaha beaches, to the east the British and Canadians were to disembark on Gold, Juno and Sword. On either flank the airborne troops, already deployed and in action, were to protect the landings.

Whilst paratroopers were being dropped over the Cotentin peninsula and along the Orne, dozens of Lancaster bombers and Flying Fortresses dropped strips of aluminum foil between Amiens and the German border to interfere with German radar. These "Windows", as they were known, played an important part in distracting the German Luftwaffe and helped to keep the Normandy skies free of German planes. To add to the confusion, Allied bombers dropped dummies fitted up with radio transmitters in Normandy. These emitted signals ordering German fighters to Calais.

Top right : a decoy paratrooper as used over Quesnay on the night of June 5-6. It was intended to confuse the Germans as to the actual landing zones. (Militaria Magazine)

....

The information network of French Resistance played an important part in channeling intelligence to the Allies; providing reliable data on enemy defenses and fortified emplacements. (F. Bachmann)

The Role of the Resistance

Overlord actually began when the French Resistance went into action. Alerted by radio messages from London, the Resistance was aware of the imminent landings. An initial message, the first verse of Verlaine's Chant d'Automne : « *Les sanglots longs des violons de l'automne...* » was followed by a second message on June 5 of the next three verses : « *Bercent mon cœur d'une langueur monotone...* ». This indicated the landings would take place within the next 48 hours.

It was a long-awaited signal and it mobilized the Resistance into spontaneous action. The day of glory had arrived. Men and women gathered in the darkness of the night and throughout France, partisans and guerrillas set to work. Over a thousand acts of sabotage were committed that night alone but resistance did not stop there. Indeed, on June 6, many members of the "Army of the Shadows" abandoned clandestine operations and began to fight in broad daylight. The Allies were concerned that disciplined action might be overwhelmed by a popular uprising, which might break free from the control of London. But they also feared that the French Resistance, whose assistance they definitely still needed, could be overwhelmed by the brutal and ruthless German repression that was sure to follow should a general revolt of the populace take place. If so, how long could the Resistance continue to keep German troops away from the frontlines?

The German air defense system situated between Cap Gris-Nez and Barfleur suffered heavily from Allied aerial attack.
(Private Collection)

The US Navy, and its British counterpart, played an important role in Operation Neptune. There were six forces deployed:
Task Force 122 (command), 124 (Force O), 125 (Force U), 126 (Force B), 127 and 128 (the Mulberry harbors).
In addition to transporting the troops and equipment from Great Britain, the naval forces also supplied the landing force with artillery cover.

Pegasus Bridge

The vanguard of the Allied force consisted of men drawn from the 82nd and 101st (US) Airborne Divisions and the British 6th Airborne Division. They were transported to Normandy in a vast aerial armada: 1,500 transport planes and gliders. The first wave consisted of pathfinders, elite reconnaissance personnel trained to mark out landing sites. The men of the 6th Airborne were destined to land between the Orne and the Dives in order to protect the flank of the men landing at Sword Beach. To do this they had to blow up five bridges over the Dives between Troarn and the coast, seize the bridges over the Orne and the Caen canal between Bénouville and Ranville, and neutralize the battery at Merville.

It was around midnight when the first six gliders circled over Caen. Their occupants, some 200 men, had been tasked with securing two bridges close to Bénouville. Pathfinders had marked out a landing strip and the first glider landed on the canal's left bank not far from the bridge that would go down in history as Pegasus Bridge. Two more gliders landed nearby. A small German force guarded the bridge and although quickly dispersed, it managed to kill the officer in charge of the attack. The battle lasted ten minutes and the British soon secured the bridge and defused German explosives which had been attached to it. The second bridge, undefended, was taken without loss. A landing site was then prepared for the second wave, two brigades of 2,000 men, which landed at 00.50 close to Ranville, a mile from Pegasus. One battalion was sent to reinforce the bridges whilst a second was sent to block the road to the east. A third was sent to prepare a further landing

zone, stripping it of its anti-glider obstacles, and making it passable for the Division's jeeps and heavy equipment. Ranville itself was quickly occupied and became the first mainland village in France to be liberated (the first French villages to be freed were in Corsica, liberated in 1943).

Meanwhile the 3rd Brigade, which had been given the mission of blowing the bridges over the Dives, met with less success. Landing sites had been poorly marked. Some pilots confused the Dives with the Orne whilst others, hit by German anti-aircraft fire, were forced to alter course. Dozens of paratroopers landed wide of their target, some as far as 16 miles away. Nevertheless, those who managed to land and regroup destroyed four of the bridges. Two of them, those at Varaville and Robehomme, were demolished by a Canadian battalion. The fifth bridge, at Troarn, was finally knocked out by an audacious group of nine men. They sped through the village in a jeep, destroyed the bridge and disappeared into the night. At 03.30, 60 transport planes successfully landed to the east of the Orne but a few crashed, killing 71 men.

The Merville Battery

There was just one more mission to accomplish, that entrusted to the 9th Parachute Battalion. The Merville battery, protected by its minefields, had to be seized. Bombers had attempted to knock it out but had only succeeded in destroying the neighboring village. The battalion's commander, Lieutenant-Colonel Terence Otway, had just 150 men with which to complete his mission. Five gliders, carrying anti-tank guns, had snapped their

A bove : Lieutenant-Colonel Otway of 6th Airborne Division. He and his men had trained for two months in preparation for their mission to seize the Merville Battery. (DR)

B ritish glider pilot . As part of the Glider Pilot Regiment, he brought over the first wave of shock troops to Normandy. (Militaria Magazine)

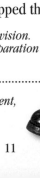

cables and crashed into the sea; others, hit by German Flak, had been blown off course and 555 paratroopers found themselves scattered up to fifty miles away. A few, unfortunately, drowned in the Dives marshes. Otway lacked any kind of heavy equipment and had just one machine-gun and few explosives. Undeterred, he pressed on with his mission. Cutting their way through the barbed wire, two groups opened the assault. The first hit the German defenders dug-in around the battery whilst the second took on the battery itself. The struggle over, the British were surprised to discover that the battery's guns consisted of some 100mm Czech cannon quite out of range of the landing beaches. Otway lost 70 killed and wounded, the Germans 178.

German Worries

It was one o'clock on the morning of June 6 and General Erich Marcks, commander of the 84th Army Corps (Army Group B) was getting ready for bed after celebrating his birthday at Saint-Lô. As he was doing so, he was informed by the commander of the 716th Infantry Division that British paratroopers had landed east of the Orne. He promptly reacted and at 02.15, the entire 7th Army was on alert. German commanders, led astray by Allied disinformation, were expecting a landing in the Pas-de-Calais, and few officers believed that a landing was now underway. The 7th Army's chief-of-staff, General Max Pemsel, was in this minority and so he contacted Rommel's chief-of-staff, Generalmajor Hans Speidel. Rommel himself was absent. Although commander of German forces in Normandy he was in fact 500 miles away, celebrating his wife's birthday at his home in Herrlingen in Germany. Speidel, meanwhile, was not convinced that an Allied landing was underway. Rommel had believed that any date for a landing had to be one on which dawn and high-water coincided and that good weather was a prerequisite. The slight improvement in the weather experienced on June 5 did not seem to shake the Germans out of their complacency. As far Allied paratroopers were concerned, he dismissed Pemsel's assertion "Perhaps you spotted some seagulls" he quipped. Even so Speidel contacted Generalfeldmarschall Gerd Von Rundstedt, commander-in-chief of forces in the west, at Saint-Germain-en-Laye. Von Rundstedt was a man famous for his decisiveness. But now even he remained cautious. Only when reports came in that engines could be heard off the Seine estuary did he begin to act. At 04.30 he placed the 12th Panzer Division (Hitlerjugend), stationed between Dreux and Louviers, and the Panzer Lehr Division, stationed between Orleans and Caen, on alert. Unbeknown to him, just fifteen minutes earlier, the first Allied troops had climbed into their landing craft and were heading towards Omaha Beach. He also sent a telegram to OKW (Wehrmacht High Command) asking for official permission to act:

A British No 4 Mark I* rifle. This rifle, together with the Bren LMG and the Sten were standard issue to British airborne troops. (Militaria Magazine)

A German Army officer's cap. A number of German officers had left their units just 4 hours before D-Day and were traveling to Rennes to take part in a Kriegspiel (wargame). (Militaria Magazine)

6TH AIRBORNE DIVISION
JUNE 5-6, 1944

SWORD BEACH

Cabourg

Ouistreham

Franceville-Plage

Merville

St-Aubin d'Arquenay

6 paras

9 paras

3 paras

Varaville

Biéville-Beuville

12 paras

1 para

Biéville-sur-Orne

Pont "Pegasus"

Blainville-sur-Orne

5 paras

Le Mesnil

711

Bricqueville

7th ARMY (Dollmann)

Lebisey

Hérouvillette

6 paras

Bois de Bavent

15th ARMY (Salmuth)

Ste-Honorine

Escoville

Bures

St-Richer

CAEN

21

K

8 paras

Sannerville

Troarn

V	Landing zones
	Destroyed batteries
	Destroyed bridges
	Bridges seized
	Areas of German resistance

'If we are now facing a large landing operation, OB-West (High Command in the West) is well aware that only an immediate response will meet with success and that this must involve the use of all available strategic reserves: the 12th SS and the Panzer Lehr. If these are brought forward at once and without delay, they will be able to participate in the fighting on the coast.'

But nobody at OKW realized the importance of this message. Hitler was asleep as was Generaloberst Alfred Jodl, head of OKH (Army High Command). Jodl, upon waking, was informed of the

The Allies made use of new identification symbols on their aircraft and gliders for the invasion. The marks, primarily bands of black and white, were termed 'invasion stripes'. Their purpose was to readily identify Allied aircraft to their own anti-aircraft batteries and other Allied pilots.

situation and he expressly forbade the use of the armored division without Hitler's authorization. The armored divisions stayed put.

American Paratroopers Enter the Fray

The American airborne divisions were given the task of securing roads and bridges in the hinterland of Utah Beach, thus permitting the landing troops to move inland as rapidly as possible. At about 01.00 waves of C-47 Skytrains (nicknamed Dakotas) flew over the Normandy coast. On board were some 13,000 men belonging to Major General Matthew B. Ridgway's 82nd Airborne Division and Major General Maxwell D. Taylor's 101st Airborne Division. This latter division was, apart from securing communications, also given the mission of neutralizing the Saint-Martin-de-Varreville batteries, as well as establishing pockets of resistance north of Carentan. The men of the 82nd had been ordered to seize the crossroads at Sainte-Mère-Eglise and establish themselves in the marshy plains to the west of the town, thus pinning down German forces based around Pont l'Abbé and Saint-Sauveur le Vicomte. If possible the 82nd was also to secure a path through

Top: American airborne troops identification flag, worn on the combat jacket sleeve.
(Militaria Magazine)

Right: rear view of an American paratrooper. The complicated parachute harness, combined with all the heavy equipment carried by the paratrooper, severely restricted movement.
(Reconstruction by Militaria Magazine)

to the west coast of the
Cotentin peninsula. Unfortunately, many of the transports
were dispersed and nearly three-quarters of the men were dropped
too far from their objectives to play any major part in these operations. Scattered across the countryside in isolated bands, these
men confused the Germans and made them unsure as to where
the forces they were opposing were. The paratroopers were able
to recognize each other by the sound of metal clickers, although
the Germans soon learned to imitate the sound and thereby killed
off a fair number of Americans. In short, Taylor could only muster
some 1,000 men and things were just as bad for the 82nd Division
five miles to the west. The 82nd had been dropped into the midst
of the German 91st Infantry Division. Two American regiments had
been ordered to blow up the bridges over the River Douve and
establish themselves along the River Merderet. But these rivers had
burst their banks and had transformed the entire area into a vast
swamp. Many paratroopers, weighed down by their equipment,
met their deaths in this watery tomb.

A street in Sainte-Mère-Eglise after the fighting. (National Archives)

German shoulder boards belonging to a member of a Luftwaffe Flak unit, and for armoured infantry. (JB Collection)

....

American specialists charged with destroying German coastal defenses often came across German "Goliaths". These devices, loaded with explosives, were remote controlled bombs. However, following the initial bombardment, the mechanisms of these devices failed. (Private Collection)

The main objective remained Sainte-Mère-Eglise and 160 men of the 505th Paratroop Infantry Regiment (82nd Airborne) were dropped into the town at 04.30 and seized the place after chasing out a flak unit. By the evening of June 6, some 15 paratroopers were killed or wounded.

Operations in the American Zone

Major-General Raymond O. Barton's 4th Division was to land on Utah Beach. The first wave was to consist of twenty landing craft and these vessels were to be supported by an aerial and naval bombardment rained down on elements of the German 709th Infantry Division commanded by Generalleutnant Karl Wilhelm von Schlieben. A patrol boat and an LCT carrying four amphibious tanks hit mines, but at 06.31, just after low tide, the first craft reached the beach and deposited 300 men of the 8th Infantry Regiment into the shallow sea. The men waded through the water as quickly as they could and got in amongst the obstacles littering the beach. The only fortifications as such were blockhouses W4, W5 and W7 perched on a low cliff.

The defenses in this sector were particularly weak primarily because the Germans relied on the flooding of the surrounding area to deter a landing, making, they thought, the establishment of a defensive line unnecessary. The landing itself was only hindered by a few problems: a patrol boat guiding the fleet of landing craft in hit a mine and, after some confusion, had to follow another to the beach. Amphibious tanks were launched too close to the shoreline creating a delay which upset the assault wave and increased the risk of collision with the nearby landing craft. As a result of all this, the flotilla set the infantry down a half mile further south from the intended point of disembarkation. They found themselves at the foot of the Audouville-la-Hubert sand dunes. Brigadier General Theodore Roosevelt, nephew of the US President, was one of the first ashore and he gathered in some 700 men.

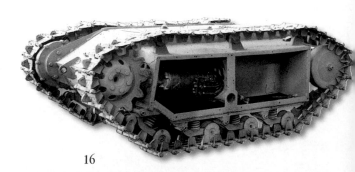

Shoulder patch for the 4th American Infantry Division. (Militaria Magazine)

By 07.00, supported by 32 amphibious tanks, he was ready to launch an attack on blockhouse W5. Luckily a direct followed by a decisive assault on the position completely knocked it out and the Americans were able to occupy it after relatively little resistance. The garrisons in the other forts, shaken by the bombardment and demoralized, put up token resistance and the fighting was over by 07.30. Soon thousands of men and vehicles were pouring ashore onto Utah Beach, with Roosevelt sticking to his new position rather than utilizing the part of the beach originally intended.

In just one hour after the first landings, sappers had marked out routes for the disembarkation of further waves of men. After just two hours tanks began to deploy along the mile-long front and began to probe forward in an attempt to join up with the paratroopers of the 101st Airborne Division. By the time the Germans became aware of the scale of the landings it was already too late as the Allies were already well established. Blockhouses were knocked out one after the other and, although there were a few pockets of resistance, most Germans chose to retreat. The artillery forts at Azeville and Saint-Marcouf formed the basis for more determined resistance but, by dusk, some 23,250 men and 1,700 vehicles were ashore. Some 197 men had been killed and 60 were missing, most likely drowned.

Right: an American assault infantryman. He wears the cotton work uniform impregnated against vesicant gases. (Militaria Magazine)

Below: Allied landing craft circle in formation before making a run for the invasion beaches. (National Archives)

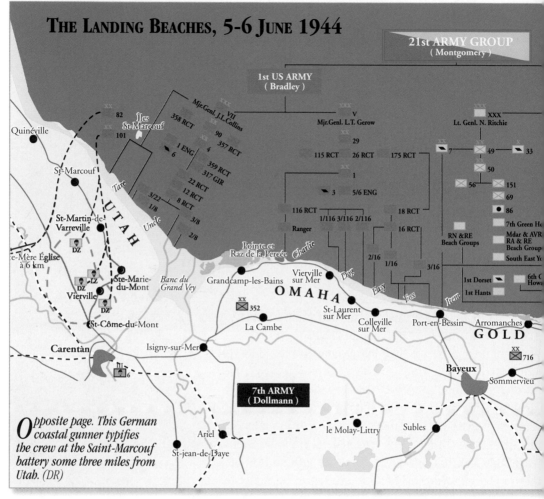

The Landing Beaches, 5-6 June 1944

21st ARMY GROUP
(Montgomery)

1st US ARMY
(Bradley)

Mjr.Genl. J.L.Collins — XXX — VII

Mjr.Genl. L.T. Gerow — XXX — V

Lt. Genl. N. Ritchie — XXX — XXX

Quinéville

Îles St-Marcouf

82

101

358 RCT

90

357 RCT

1 ENG

6

4

359 RCT

317 GIR

22 RCT

12 RCT

8 RCT

3/22

1/8

St-Marcouf

Tare

UTAH

St-Martin-de-Varreville

Uncle

3/8

2/8

DZ

e-Mère Église
à 6 km

LZ

DZ

Ste-Marie-du-Mont

Banc du Grand Vey

Vierville

DZ

St-Côme-du-Mont

Carentan

Isigny-sur-Mer

6

Grandcamp-les-Bains

Pointe et Raz de la Percée

La Cambe

352

Charlie

OMAHA

Vierville sur Mer

St-Laurent sur Mer

Dog

Easy

Fox

Colleville sur Mer

115 RCT   26 RCT   175 RCT

29

1

116 RCT   5/6 ENG

3

1/116 3/116 2/116

Ranger

18 RCT

16 RCT

2/16

1/16

3/16

7

49

33

50

56   151

69

86

7th Green He

Mdar & AVR
RA & RE
Beach Group

South East Yo

6th C
Howa

1st Dorset

1st Hants

RN &RE
Beach Groups

Port-en-Bessin

Arromanches

GOLD

Bayeux

716

Sommervieu

Subles

le Molay-Littry

Ariel

St-jean-de-Daye

7th ARMY
(Dollmann)

Opposite page. This German coastal gunner typifies the crew at the Saint-Marcouf battery some three miles from Utah. (DR)

Below : the battery at Saint-Marcouf came under fire from American cruisers at dawn on June 6. It hit back, damaging a number of US ships. (National Archives)

Omaha Beach

The landings at Utah had fortunately been an outright success. It was not to be the same with those at Omaha. This beach, flanked by high cliffs, was a bad choice. Behind the German defenses there were marshy flats crossed by four roads heading inland.

The beach itself was covered with obstacles: iron girders and wooden stakes. Barbed wire criss-crossed the dunes whilst bunkers armed with 75mm and 88mm guns dominated the beach. Indeed there were 35 block-houses, eight pits for heavy artillery, 18 for anti-tank guns and 85 machine gun nests.

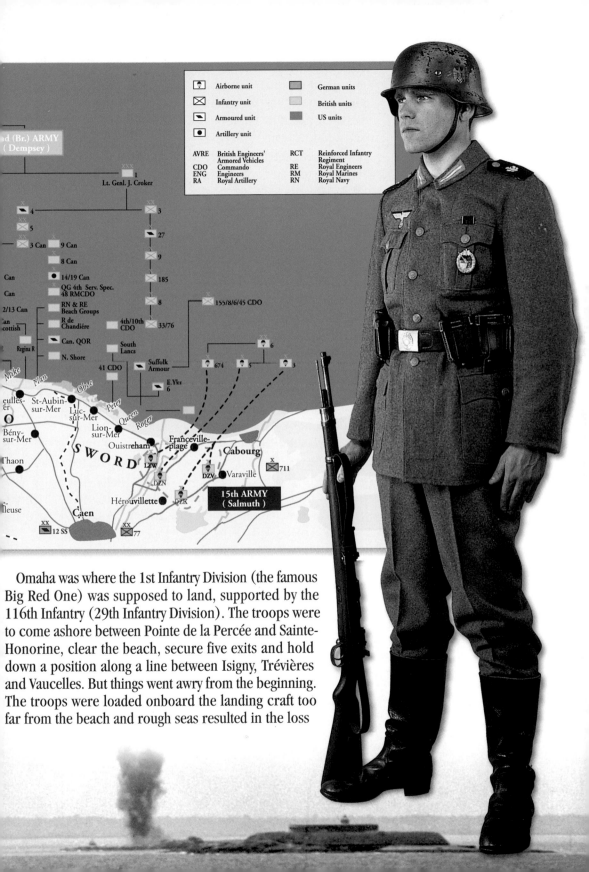

Map legend

Airborne unit		German units	
Infantry unit		British units	
Armoured unit		US units	
Artillery unit			

AVRE	British Engineers' Armored Vehicles	RCT	Reinforced Infantry Regiment
CDO	Commando	RE	Royal Engineers
ENG	Engineers	RM	Royal Marines
RA	Royal Artillery	RN	Royal Navy

ad (Br.) ARMY
(Dempsey)

XXX
I
Lt. Genl. J. Croker

4
5
3 Can · 9 Can
Can · 8 Can
Can · 14/19 Can
QG 4th Serv. Spec.
48 RMCDO
2/13 Can
'an cottish · RN & RE Beach Groups
R de Chandiére
Regina R · Can. QOR
N. Shore
41 CDO

3
27
9
185
8
155/8/6/45 CDO
4th/10th CDO · 33/76
South Lancs
Suffolk Armour
E. Yks

674   5   3
6

Mike   Nan   Obuc   Peter   Queen   Roger

eulles-er
St-Aubin-sur-Mer
Luc-sur-Mer
Bény-sur-Mer
Lion-sur-Mer
Ouistreham
Franceville-plage
Cabourg
Thon
S W O R D   LZW
DZN   Varaville
DZV
Hérouvillette   DZK

15th ARMY
(Salmuth)

711

Ileuse   Caen
12 SS   77

Omaha was where the 1st Infantry Division (the famous Big Red One) was supposed to land, supported by the 116th Infantry (29th Infantry Division). The troops were to come ashore between Pointe de la Percée and Sainte-Honorine, clear the beach, secure five exits and hold down a position along a line between Isigny, Trévières and Vaucelles. But things went awry from the beginning. The troops were loaded onboard the landing craft too far from the beach and rough seas resulted in the loss

of 10 boats. As each carried 30 men, some 300 troops were pitched into the cold waters, weighed down by equipment, and many drowned as a consequence. Equipment too was lost, some 26 guns sinking to the bottom. The amphibious tanks fared little better. They began their assault five miles from the shore and of the 29 DD's some 24 were defeated by the rough seas, sinking with their crews, one was hit by a landing craft and two were destroyed by enemy fire. Fortunately an attack by heavy bombers of the 8th Air Force did something to restore morale during this trying episode. But, despite its spectacular nature, this air raid accomplished little. Some 13,000 bombs fell into the marshes behind the beaches, throwing up smoke which impeded the naval bombardment then in progress. The Germans were now well and truly prepared. Their artillery batteries, positioned five miles behind the beaches bided their time, waiting for the order to come to open fire.

The troops destined to make the landing assumed they would just be facing the 716th Infantry Division composed of ethnic Germans from Poland and Russian ex-POWs of dubious value. But, unknown

The death notice for a Luftwaffe non-commissioned officer killed on June 6 in Normandy. (R. Theys Collection)

to them, these men were supported by elements of the 352nd Infantry Division, combat seasoned veterans transferred from the Eastern Front to Saint-Lô just a couple of weeks beforehand. They were already trained in how to resist an amphibious landing.

The 116th Regiment was the first American infantry unit to attempt to land on the western part of the beach. At 06.36 as the landing craft ramps were lowered, the Americans found themselves caught in the cross-fire of machineguns and hit by mortars and artillery. The confusion was horrible and hundreds of men became casualties. Those who survived the inferno, and who didn't drown, attempted to wade ashore. But the beach was so encumbered with obstacles that most men were forced back into the water. A few men made it behind a low defensive line halfway up the beach and sheltered there. Meanwhile successive waves were hitting the beach, choking it with more men, corpses and destroyed equipment. Engineers, who came ashore at 07.30, attempted to open up paths through the obstacles. In theory they could destroy seven of these beach obstacles in 27 minutes but, on the ground, it proved impossible to destroy even one in the allotted time. Five other paths were opened before the tide turned. The land-

Shoulder patch for separate American tank battalions. (Militaria Magazine)

....

An American Duplex Drive amphibious Sherman tank (British adaptation). Classed as a secret weapon at the time, it had a flotation skirt and two propellers with which it could achieve a speed of around four miles an hour over a calm sea. (National Archives)

ing craft themselves were frequently hit by artillery or mines.

The Ghost Batteries of Pointe du Hoc

Four miles to the west of Omaha, 225 men of the 2nd Ranger Battalion under Lieutenant Colonel James E. Rudder landed beneath the cliffs of the Pointe du Hoc. On top of these cliffs was supposed to be the most impressive battery in this sector of the coast, equipped with six 155mm guns each with a range of 15 miles. The battery had already been pounded by the American warships *Texas* and *Arkansas*, as well as hit by air raids, but, it seemed, had largely escaped damage.

The Rangers were unable to use their DUKW's, especially equipped with firemen's ladders, as the coastline was riddled with craters, so the men had to resort to using rope ladders and grappling hooks. The ascent began under the fire of 200 men of the German 716th Infantry Division defending the battery. A number of Rangers were hit and fell to the ground. Fortunately, two destroyers, *USS Satterlee* and *HMS Talybont*, arrived off the coast in support and opened up an accurate and devastating fire on the battery. This intervention allowed the Rangers to reach the summit and seize the battery, taking the survivors of the garrison prisoner. But they now discovered they had been the victims of a cruel

Top left. Should-er patch for American Engineer Special Brigades. They, along with the naval assault teams, played a key part in Overlord by allowing the free flow of men and equipment on the Invasion beaches.
(JG Collection)

....

A copy of the 'Dobrovolets' (Volunteer) newspaper issued on 12 May 1944. It was produced for former Soviet prisoners of war serving in the German Army. There were three such battalions serving in Normandy. (DR)

....

These two GIs have struck a martial pose. They wear assault jackets, only partially issued to infantry in the first wave. (National Archives)

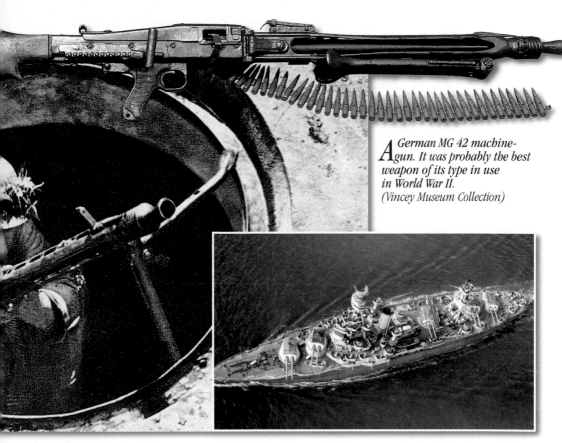

A German MG 42 machine-gun. It was probably the best weapon of its type in use in World War II. (Vincey Museum Collection)

deception. There were no guns, merely gun carriages bearing telephone poles. The gun barrels were later discovered hidden in a barn inland. The Rangers held the position for two days, beating off numerous counterattacks, but this single operation cost them some 138 men.

Bloody Omaha

Meanwhile, at 10.30, some 200 men of the 116th Regiment's 1st battalion had taken advantage of the smoke pouring up from burning scrub which was

The ancient cruiser USS Texas opened up on Pointe du Hoc and the coastal batteries of Vierville-sur-Mer to support the 116th US Infantry Regiment. (National Archives)

US assault jacket. It was so heavy that a number of men ditched it as soon as they hit the water to avoid drowning under its weight. (Private Collection)

On the right flank of Omaha Beach the Germans had constructed a wall some eight feet tall. It was breached and finally destroyed by engineers. (National Archives)

P ointe du Hoc following the American naval and aerial bombardment. The cliff lip has partly crumbled, making it easier for troops to clamber to the summit. (National Archives)

R angers climbing at Pointe du Hoc. Rope ladders and grappling hooks were all used in the assault. (National Archives)

A lieutenant in the US Coast Guard would have worn this M1 helmet. The Coast Guard played a vital role in the invasion, directing landing craft and picking up some 1,483 troops who otherwise would have drowned. (Le Poilu Collection)

then shrouding Omaha Beach to push forward and cut through the barbed wire on top of the dunes. They then traversed the minefields and pushed on as far as Vierville a half mile inland.

Further to the east the 2nd and 3rd battalions had also made their way through the minefields which had largely been destroyed in the preceding bombardment and were nearing Saint-Laurent. To the east of them elements of the 16th Infantry Regiment headed for Colleville, having made their way through a cleft in the cliff and braved the fire of several German positions. They then turned towards Port-en-Bessin, hoping to join up with the British. In the central sector a few troops had managed to push past the machine-gun nests and make for Colleville but the majority remained pinned down on the beach. The situation was becoming desperate as landing craft couldn't get close enough to the beach because of the debris of destroyed boats and vehicles. Throughout this time the Americans lived in dread of the arrival of German reinforcements. Rear Admiral John L. Hall, commanding Force O, charged with supporting the landings, was well aware of the dangers. To mitigate the peril he had his destroyers approach as close as possible to the coast and had them fire broadsides from every available gun, pounding the coast. At 11.00 the battle began to turn. Whilst the three surviving DD tanks opened up on the German positions, Colonel Taylor at the head of his men broke through the barbed wire and over the minefields. The 18th Infantry Regiment, freshly landed, supported him and broke through the German lines at around 12.30. Around 13.00 the last blockhouses were being subdued while sappers dismantled the defenses and let the infantry pour through. By the end of the day vehicles were moving forward, passing over the beach and heading along the road to Colleville where tanks and infantry were fighting with German defenders.

The second line of German defenses was formed along the coastal road. It was breached before sunset by the 115th and 116th Regiments of the 1st Division. Further to the west, Vierville also fell to the Americans. As night fell the Americans had 30,000 men ashore. They were squeezed into a pocket five miles long and one mile deep.

Operations in the British Zone

The sector targeted by the Anglo-Canadian forces was 25 miles wide. The beaches had been designated Gold, Juno and Sword. Following a naval bombardment, which lasted one hour, the landing craft set off for the shore some 4 miles away. The coastline, defended by the German 716th Division, although not as jagged as in the American sector, was protected by a veritable forest of barricades, ramps and mines. The first ashore were frogmen, attempting to defuse the mines and pull down the defenses. At 07.25 the first landing craft came into land, navigating their way through the defenses. A good number were destroyed: they hit mines placed atop angled stakes, were ripped open and floundered. Nevertheless, the operation proved easier than Omaha.

Gold beach

The 1st Battalion of the Royal Hampshire Regiment, part of Major General D.A.H. Graham's 50th (Northumbrian) Infantry Division, followed specially adapted tanks ashore onto Gold Beach. Their objective was to reach Bayeux and to prevent German tanks heading to the beach along the Bayeux-Caen highway. In addition they were to link up with the Americans at Port-en-Bessin, take the fortified village of Arromanches, and make the coast secure enough for one of the Mulberry harbors to become operational. But, in order to stand any chance, they first had to seize the village of Le Hamel. This was occupied by a unit of the German 352nd Division, securely dug-in in a sanatorium and supported by an 88mm gun. This gun was carefully placed so as to have a clear shot at the incoming craft. The Hampshires found themselves without cover on the beach, pinned down by machine-gun

*R*ear-Admiral Hall, commander of Force O. This Force oversaw the disembarkation of the US 1st and 29th Infantry Divisions and provided artillery support for them. *(National Archives)*

*A*British No 36 M Mills grenade. *(Private Collection)*

....

*A*number of houses assumed to have been fortified by the Germans were heavily shelled by warships. *(National Archives)*

*The equipment used by this American Martin B-26 Marauder pilot includes an A-2 flying jacket, AN-6550 flying suit, a B-4 lifejacket and A-10 flying gloves. His parachute is of the type issued to British airmen.
(Militaria Magazine)*

Above : sleeve patch worn by men of the 9th Tactical Air Force. (Militaria Magazine)

Martin B-26 Marauder bombers fly towards the Normandy coast. Such medium bombers were deployed by the 9th Tactical Air Force formed by 400 aircraft in eight groups. They were amongst the first planes to operate over Normandy at dawn on June 6 and their intended targets were the batteries around Utah Beach. (IWM)

Aerial operations

Aerial forces engaged by the Allies consisted of 15,770 aircraft of all types. Against this overwhelming force, the Luftwaffe, a shadow of its former self, only had weak forces with which to oppose this armada (just five groups of fighters in the whole of France). As a result German aerial operations against the Allies were sporadic to say the least. The Germans had the 2nd and 26th Fighter Squadrons (I et II./Jagdgeschwader 2 - I./Jagdgeschwader 26) and the 1st Group of the 10th Bomber Squadron (I./Schnellkampfgeschwader 10) in the vicinity. Even so they claimed their first victory at dawn between 05.01 and 05.04 when four Lancasters were shot down in the Isigny / Carentan sector by Focke-Wulf 190s belonging to I./SKG 10. Around 09.00 two Focke-Wulf 190s, piloted by Josef Pips Priller and NCO Wodarczyk of I./JG 26 , from Lille, strafed the beaches before disappearing, much to the relief of the British troops. A pilot from the same unit later shot down a Mustang to the south-west of Caen at 21.00 in the evening. A dozen FW 190s had attacked Gold Beach, shooting up ships and landing craft before machine-gunning the beaches. Allied fighters were also hit. The first was a P-47 Thunderbolt, hit by Major Bühligen, commander of I./JG 2, at 11.57 as it passed over the moth of the Orne. His unit shot down another Thunderbolt and eight Mustangs, only two of which were credited. The (II./JG 2), according to its own records, shot down three Typhoons at 12.10 over Caen and a further eight aircraft before the end of the day. By the evening of the 6th some 14,674 Allied sorties had taken place over France as opposed to 319 by the Luftwaffe. Some six Allied heavy bombers and 50 fighters had been reported missing, victims of enemy aircraft or Flak, the redoubtable German anti-aircraft artillery. Eleven German pilots were killed or wounded in action.

fire and mortars. Some 200 were killed. Preferring to avoid a direct assault, the British attacked Le Hamel but were mown down and soon reduced to company strength. The sanatorium was finally taken at 16.30, battered into submission by a tank equipped with a mortar.

Further to the east especially adapted tanks were able to drive inland, negotiating their way round bomb craters and anti-tank defenses whilst isolated blockhouses or fortified houses were destroyed. The 1st Dorset headed for Arromanches whilst, simultaneously, 47 (Royal Marine) Commando hit the coast to the east of Le Hamel. Port-en-Bessin was also reached. Further along the beach the 5th Battalion of the East Yorkshires and the 6th of the Green Howards quickly crossed the sands. Close cooperation between the infantry and the engineers enabled the British to take the village of La Riviere after having destroyed an 88mm. By the end of the morning a number of routes inland had been opened up and by the evening most objectives had been secured. The beachhead was five miles long and as many wide.

Juno Beach

Juno Beach was to be hit by the two brigades of Major General Rodney Keller's 3rd (Canadian) Infantry Division as well as 48 (Royal Marine) Commando. The landing area stretched five miles between the villages of La Riviere and Saint-Aubin. The weather was bad, the sappers, who should have been sent ahead to defuse the mined obstacles on the beach, were late and the infantry were sent in without initial armored support. The result was that the Germans had the opportunity to bolster their defenses and fight back. Some 90, out of 306 landing craft, were destroyed. The infantry who did manage to get ashore found themselves terribly exposed. Numerous emplacements and defensive positions delayed progress towards Bernières but, by 08.30, resistance had largely been overcome. Meanwhile, at Courselles, the Royal Winnipegs and the Regina Rifles of the 7th (Canadian) Brigade managed to break through the German defenses but their progress was impeded by the tide. At Bernières, the 8th

*G*eneral Miles Dempsey commanded the 2nd (British) Army and was, like Omar Bradley, directly subordinate to Montgomery (commander of land forces during Overlord). Montgomery respected Dempsey for his calm and thorough manner.
(IWM)

*A*British Enfield No 2 Mark I* revolver
(Militaria Magazine)

*F*ormation sign for the British 3rd Infantry Division. Evacuated at Dunkirk in 1940, it was stationed and trained in Britain until D-Day.
(Militaria Magazine)

At Lion-sur-Mer a Churchill tank specially adapted for destroying fortified positions allows a column of Bren Carriers to go by. It was capable of firing a 20kg destructive charge some 80 meters. Some 180 Churchill 'Petards' had been adapted to carry such mortars in readiness for D-Day.
(IWM)

A German steel helmet.
(Militaria Magazine)

....

C Cap badge of the Regina Rifles, part of the 7th Brigade, 3rd Canadian Division, one of the two Canadian assault formations on 6 June.
(Private Collection)

....

A Focke-Wulf 190 fighter in the livery of ace Josef Priller.
(Model built by Juan M. Villalba Dominguez/WingMasters)

(Canadian) Brigade followed the 7th but lost its tanks on the way. The Queen's Own Rifles were decimated in their attempt to get over an earthwork and only a violent assault, supported by open-sighted artillery fire, allowed the troops to move forwards. When the 9th (Canadian) Brigade, acting as a reserve, landed less than an hour later, there was considerable confusion on the beach and this delayed an effective advance for some time. But, by the end of the day, the Canadians had linked up with the British at Gold, forming a front some 14 miles long and had achieved the majority of the objectives set for them. The only jarring note was that the Canadians had not been able to contact the British on Sword Beach. 48 (Royal Marine) Commando, charged with this mission, had been frustrated by resistance based on the village of Langrune. The defenders here were securely placed behind a mass of mines and barbed wire. The village protected a route which the 21st Panzer Division intended to use as it came up from Caen to engage the British at Sword.

A Canadian poster celebrating French-Canadian solidarity with the forces of the Commonwealth. American General Patton declared that "the Canadians are Montgomery's best soldiers, because they are (North) Americans!". (DR)

Building of the artillery observation bunker at Longues-sur-Mer hadn't been completed by D-Day. Optical instruments were lacking. At the time, an earth mound would hide the observation post, to make it invisible from the sea. Each gun pit contained a 150-mm Krupp gun and, on D-Day, the battery exchanged shots with the Allied fleet. Despite the lack of range-finders, the battery hit HMS *Bulolo*. It then came under fire from the French cruisers *Montcalm* and *Georges Leygues* as well as HMS *Ajax*. The battery was silenced in the afternoon.

Rommel Gets Involved

Speidel was still convinced that the assault on Normandy was nothing more than a diversion. Given the scale of the landings, however, he was still obliged to keep Rommel informed of every development. Rommel, shaken by developments, rushed over to his headquarters at La Roche-Guyon. At 10.00 on June 6, Hitler finally woke up and was informed of the news. Without flinching he authorized von Rundstedt to make use of the two armored divisions but none of the other reserves; it was too early to tell whether or not there might be more landings elsewhere. Rommel's arrival certainly injected impetus into the German defense but vital hours had been lost. The main batteries had already been reduced to silence, access roads had been cut and bridges destroyed. Von Rundstedt's Chief of Operations, Oberst Bodo Zimmermann, wrote that "this, the first crucial day, had been lost and the success of the landings already assured". Von Rundstedt himself had his breakfast and then spent the greater part of the morning pruning roses in the gardens adjacent to his headquarters. But Generalmajor Edgar Feuchtinger's 21st Panzer Division stationed at Caen, the vital gate to the Seine and Paris, was impatient for orders to take them into action. These finally arrived around 16.00 and the division set off towards Sword, the nearest beach.

Sword

At 07.30 the 1st Battalion of the South Lancashire Regiment and the 2nd Battalion of the East Yorkshire, belonging to Major General T.G. Rennie's 3rd Infantry Division, had come ashore between Lion and La Brèche. They were supported by 25 amphibious tanks. The beach was soon secured as the assault force only being hit by sporadic fire but the incoming tide caused problems and chaos reigned. Men and equipment were restricted to an ever-narrowing beach. Only at noon did the receding tide help matters and allow the situation to improve. But the South Lancashire's had in the meantime, pressed on and chased the Germans out of Hermanville.

The pursuit took the British as far as Caen but there they ran into the 21st Panzer Division's vanguard supported by three anti-tank guns posted on an incline near Périers. The British halted and awaited the arrival of supports. These didn't show for the next three hours and tanks didn't appear until some time after that. Finally some 20 tanks were brought forward little know ing that 40 German tanks waited for them. The Germans had inserted themselves within a six-mile wide corridor, the boundary between the Juno and Sword beaches. They would then be able to breach the Allied front between Caen and the sea... The fighting began when the British assaulted the village of Lebisey, forcing the Germans back to Biéville. However the German tanks had gone into action, attacking Périers, but losing 7 tanks, before reaching Luc-sur-Mer at 20.00. Here the forward units awaited reinforcements. But German plans were interrupted by a low-altitude air raid which sowed confusion. The Germans, fearing that gliders had landed paratroopers in their rear, and that these had cut their retreat, pulled back their tanks.

Commandos in Action

Brigadier General Lord Lovat's 1st Special Service Brigade landed on Sword between 08.45 and 09.20. It was composed of 3, 4, 6 and 45 Commandos. In addition, Brigadier B.W. Leicester's 4th Special Service Brigade (Commandos 41 and 46) and Colonel Robert Dawson's 4 Commando also came ashore at La Brèche at 08.20. The 177 Frenchmen in this Commando, commanded by Free French Navy Lieutenant Philippe Kieffer, joined their British comrades in the push towards Riva-Bella, seizing a few entrenchments around the old casino. The Commandos joined up with the Paras from Pegasus Bridge and acted as liaison between them and the troops just landed. 46 Commando seized Luc-sur-Mer.

The Cost

By the evening of the June 6, it was clear that the landings had been a success even though that success had not yet been consolidated. The Atlantic Wall had been breached. Everything had exceeded expectations and the decoy operation carried out against the Luftwaffe meant that the invasion had taken place beneath skies devoid of German aircraft. Despite near disaster at Omaha, casualties had been less than those predicted at Allied HQ. Casualties had been heavy (12,000 killed, wounded or missing) but

A private of the British 50th (Northumbrian) Division.
(Reconstruction by Militaria Magazine)

nothing like the 75,000 predicted had Neptune failed to surprise the Germans. In all 152,000 men had set foot on German defended soil. All that was left was to link up all the disparate forces. Even so, perhaps the worst was to come. For Hitler could order Plan III, the deployment of the entire 15th Army's reserves. This mass of armor could roll forward and drive the Allies back into the water if they didn't consolidate their position quickly. The outcome of the campaign was still in the balance.

PRACTICAL INFORMATION

Normandy is a region rich in museums, war cemeteries and memorials. There are indeed so many that it is impossible to present them all here. This is a selection focused on sites located in the actual landing zones of June 6. These are all found in the Calvados district. Details of museums found inland, concerning operations conducted at a later date, can be found in other mini-guides.

The itinerary begins in **Caen** at the **Mémorial de la Paix**. Here exhibits give an overall view of the war. The origins of the conflict are explained by footage presented on screens sunk into the walls; these images are drawn from contemporary newsreels and cover the Nuremberg rallies, Hitler's speeches, General de Gaulle's appeal, the Occupation, the consequences of war, etc.

Mémorial pour la Paix
Esplanade Dwight Eisenhower
BP 6261 - 14066 Caen CEDEX 4
Tel.: 02 31 06 06 44 - fax: 02 31 06 06 70
www.unicaen.fr/memorial
Email: memorial@unicaen.fr

Open every day from 09.00 to 19.00; 09.00 to 20.00 in summer; 09.00 to 18.00 in winter. Closed for the first two weeks of January and December 25.

The **museum of the Merville Battery** is twelve miles to the north-east of Caen and is based around four of the casemates which came under fire. A tour around the buildings gives an excellent impression of the defenses. The exhibit itself is inside one of the defenses and it shows the history of the battery, uniforms, equipment, weapons and artifacts, as well as a rich collection of photos.

Musée de la batterie de Merville
14810 Merville
Tel. / fax: 02 31 91 47 53

Opening hours:
10.00 to 17.30 from March 1 to May 31
10.00 to 18.00 from June to the end of September
10.00 to 17.30 from October to November 11

Groups can be allowed access outside of season, contact the museum to make a reservation. French-speaking and English-speaking guides are available.

Five miles from Merville is the **Pegasus Memorial** at Ranville-Bénouville dedicated to the men of 6th Airborne. Information on the division's mission, including the capture of the Bénouville Bridge, is presented as are numerous artifacts from the fighting. Archival films are shown and the museum, as well as the original Pegasus Bridge itself, form part of a park.

Mémorial Pegasus - Musée des troupes aéroportées britanniques
Avenue du Major Howard
14860 Ranville
Tel.: 02 31 78 19 44 - fax: 02 31 78 19 42
Email: memorial.pegasus@wanadoo.fr

Opening from February 1 to December 15.
Closed December 16 to January 31
In summer opening hours are 9.30 to 18.30.

Four miles from the Pegasus Memorial, not far from the beach at Ouistreham, is the **Atlantic Wall Museum**. This is located in a vast bunker, the former HQ commanding all the batteries along the Orne estuary. It gives the visitor a real insight into the way such defenses functioned. The rooms are on five levels and have been fitted out just as they were during the war. There are boiler rooms, sleeping quarters, a pharmacy, a hospital, magazines, communication rooms and an observation post fitted with a powerful range-finder.

Musée du bunker du Mur de l'Atlantique
Boulevard du 6 juin
14150 Ouistreham-Riva-Bella
Tel.: 02 31 97 28 69 - fax: 02 31 96 66 05
Email: bunkermusée@aol.com

Opening hours:
10.00 to 18.00 from February 3 to November 15
09.00 to 19.00 from April 1 to September 30
Closed November 16 to February 2.

Five miles to the east of Ouistreham, at Douvres-la-Delivrande, is the **Würzburg-Riese Radar Museum**. This evokes this key installation, charged with monitoring the Channel and the skies for enemy movement. Some 250 Luftwaffe personnel formed the garrison here. The museum, housed in a casemate, displays the only such radar in the whole of France.

Musée du radar Würzburg-Riese
Route Basly
14440 Douvres-la-Délivrande
Tel.: 02 31 37 74 43
(Groups telephone 02 31 06 06 45)

Open between July 6 to August 31, 10.00 to 18.00.

Fifteen miles from Douvres, near Arromanches, is the **America-Gold Beach museum**. This belongs to the Association des Sites et Musées de la bataille de Normandie. There are two buildings and exhibits describe the landings as well as the role of the 50th Division in King sector, Gold Beach.

Musée America-Gold Beach
2, place Amiral Byrd
14114 Ver-sur-Mer
Tel. / fax: 02 31 22 58 58

Opening hours:
From 10.30 to 13.30 and 14.30 to 17.30 in July and August.
Wednesdays and Thursdays (09.30 to 12.00) from November 1 to April 30. Closed Tuesdays in May, June, September and October.

Right in amongst the landing beaches is the **Arromanches Museum**, built by the site of the Mulberry harbor. The diorama, models, films and exhibits cover the whole of Operation Overlord.

Musée du débarquement d'Arromanches
Place du 6 juin
14117 Arromanches
Tel.: 02 31 22 34 31 - fax: 02 31 92 68 83
www.normandy1944.com

Open all year round (except January):
from 10.00 to 12.30 and 13.30 to 17.00.
In summer opening hours are 09.00 to 19.00.

In the same town can be seen the **Arromanches 360° Museum**. This shows a film, the Price of Liberty, on a panoramic screen. It plunges the viewer right into the heart of D-Day.

Musée Arromanches 360°
Chemin du Calvaire - BP 9
14117 Arromanches
Tel.: 02 31 22 30 30 - fax: 02 31 22 33 55